4/16

ROBOTICS

Lynn Peppas

CRABTREE
Publishing Company
www.crabtreebooks.com

Crabtree Publishing Company
www.crabtreebooks.com

Author: Lynn Peppas

**Publishing plan research
and development**: Reagan Miller

Editors: Rachel Minay, Kathy Middleton

Proofreader: Wendy Scavuzzo

Photo Researcher: Rachel Minay/Lynn Peppas

Original design: Tim Mayer
(Mayer Media)

Book design: Clare Nicholas

Cover design: Ken Wright

**Production coordinator and
prepress tecnician**: Ken Wright

Print coordinator: Katherine Berti

Produced for Crabtree Publishing
Company by White-Thomson Publishing

Cover:
Shutterstock: produktionsbuero TINUS (top left)
Wikimedia: Das Foto wurde vom FZI
freigegeben (bottom left); Humanrobo
(bottom right)

Photographs:
Corbis: Erik Tham: pp. 16–17; George
Steinmetz: p. 36; ISSEI KATO/Reuters:
pp. 34–35; John Zich/zrImages: p. 33;
LEONHARD FOEGER/Reuters: pp. 38–39;
SHENG LI/Reuters: pp. 14–15; **Dreamstime:**
Martin Brayley: p. 42; Mellowbox: pp.
22–23; **Getty Images:** Time & Life Pictures:
p. 40; Mary Evans Picture Library: p.
18; **Shutterstock:** AlexanderZam: p. 20t;
Betastock: p. 1; Boris15: p. 20b; Buravtsoff:
pp. 44–45; Denis Tabler: pp. 4–5; DM7: p.
37; higyou: p. 41; James J. Flanigan: p. 32;
James Steidl: pp. 24–25; megastocker: p. 11;
ndoeljindoel: p. 13; RTimages: p. 12; s_bukley:
p. 19; Stefano Tinti: p. 3; SuperStock: Science
and Society: p. 8; **Thinkstock:** Andreas
Meyer: p. 24; Kim Steele: p. 10; Stocktrek
Images: p. 21; **Topfoto:** The Granger
Collection: p. 9; Vecna: pp. 28–29; **Wikimedia:**
pp. 4, 6, 26, 43; Clemens Vasters: pp. 30–31;
Enfo: p. 7l; Outisnn: p. 27; Rama: p. 7r.

Library and Archives Canada Cataloguing in Publication

Peppas, Lynn, author
        Robotics / Lynn Peppas.

(Crabtree chrome)
Includes index.
Issued in print and electronic formats.
ISBN 978-0-7787-1369-2 (bound).--ISBN 978-0-7787-1405-7 (pbk.).--
ISBN 978-1-4271-8982-0 (pdf).--ISBN 978-1-4271-8976-9 (html)

        1. Robots--Juvenile literature. I. Title. II. Series: Crabtree
chrome

TJ213.5.P47 2014   j629.8'92   C2014-903919-0
                                             C2014-903920-4

Library of Congress Cataloging-in-Publication Data

Peppas, Lynn, author.
  Robotics / Lynn Peppas.
      pages cm -- (Crabtree Chrome)
  Includes index.
  ISBN 978-0-7787-1369-2 (reinforced library binding) --
ISBN 978-0-7787-1405-7 (pbk.) --
ISBN 978-1-4271-8982-0 (electronic pdf) --
ISBN 978-1-4271-8976-9 (electronic html)
  1. Robots--Juvenile literature. 2. Robotics--Juvenile
literature. I. Title.

TJ211.2.P47 2015
629.8'92--dc23

                                             2014027807

Crabtree Publishing Company
www.crabtreebooks.com   1-800-387-7650

Printed in the U.S.A./092014/JA20140811

Published in Canada
Crabtree Publishing
616 Welland Ave.
St. Catharines, ON
L2M 5V6

Published in the United States
Crabtree Publishing
PMB 59051
350 Fifth Avenue, 59th Floor
New York, New York 10118

Published in the United Kingdom
Crabtree Publishing
Maritime House
Basin Road North, Hove
BN41 1WR

Published in Australia
Crabtree Publishing
3 Charles Street
Coburg North
VIC 3058

Contents

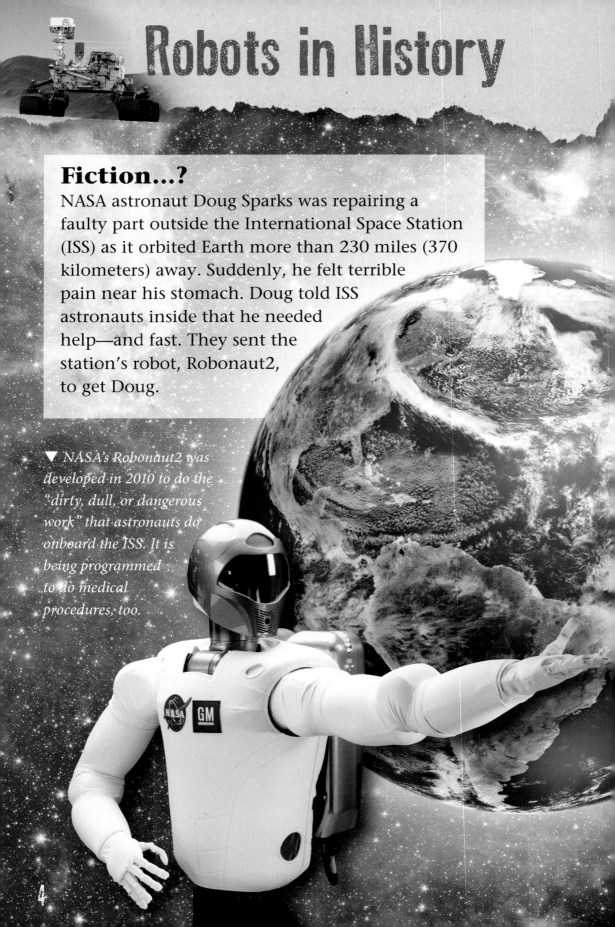

Fiction...?

NASA astronaut Doug Sparks was repairing a faulty part outside the International Space Station (ISS) as it orbited Earth more than 230 miles (370 kilometers) away. Suddenly, he felt terrible pain near his stomach. Doug told ISS astronauts inside that he needed help—and fast. They sent the station's robot, Robonaut2, to get Doug.

▼ NASA's Robonaut2 was developed in 2010 to do the "dirty, dull, or dangerous work" that astronauts do onboard the ISS. It is being programmed to do medical procedures, too.

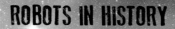

...Or Future Fact?

Robonaut2 brought Doug back inside and **diagnosed** him as having appendicitis. Doug needed emergency surgery or he would die. Robonaut2 prepared Doug for surgery. A surgical robot, called da Vinci, performed it successfully. Doug's life was saved in space by robots. This story isn't completely true—surgery has not been performed in space yet—but it could be in the very near future!

The surgical robot, da Vinci, was designed in 2000 to perform battlefield surgery from a distance. Today, da Vinci performs surgery (on Earth) with the guidance of human surgeons miles away.

diagnosed: found out what was wrong with someone

Imagining Robots Long Ago

Almost 3,000 years ago, a Greek poet named Homer imagined what life would be like with robots. In a poem called the *Iliad*, he wrote about female servant robots made of gold. Many centuries later, the famous Italian artist and inventor Leonardo da Vinci invented a robotic knight in the late 1400s. Da Vinci's knight could sit, stand, move its head, and lift its face shield.

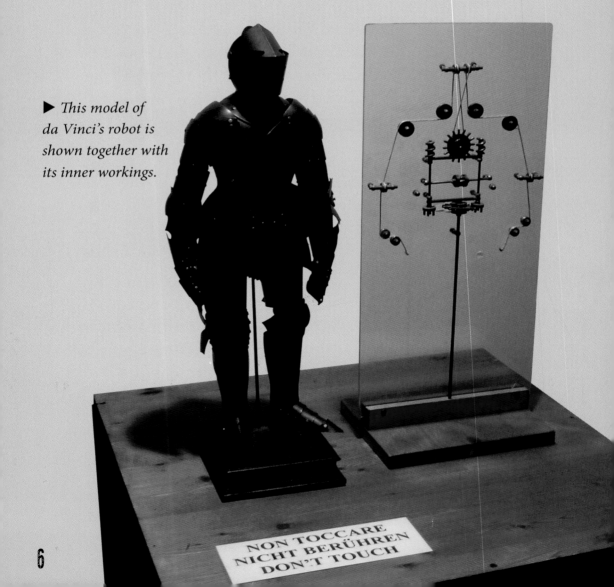

▶ *This model of da Vinci's robot is shown together with its inner workings.*

NON TOCCARE
NICHT BERÜHREN
DON'T TOUCH

Automata

Da Vinci's invention is called an **automaton**.
In 1773, Pierre and Henri-Louis Jaquet-Droz also
made automata in the forms of a woman playing
a piano, a young child that draws four different
pictures, and another that writes up to 40 letters.

◀▼ *Although they look
like robots, automata are
not really considered to be
robots because they cannot
sense their surroundings.*

The word "robot" was first
used in the 1920s in Czech
playwright Karel Capek's
play *Rossum's Universal
Robots*. The Czech word,
robota, means "forced
work" in English.

automaton: a moving machine, often in the shape of a human

The First Step

In 1948, a tortoise robot created by American inventor William Grey Walter turned what had once only been imagined, one step closer to reality. Walter's tortoise was special because it had **sensors**. It reacted to light and avoided anything in its way. It seemed to think and move on its own.

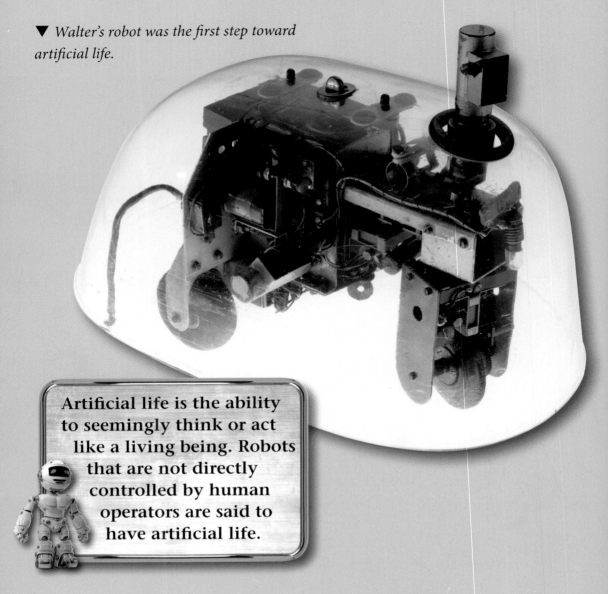

▼ *Walter's robot was the first step toward artificial life.*

Artificial life is the ability to seemingly think or act like a living being. Robots that are not directly controlled by human operators are said to have artificial life.

Getting Closer

In 1954, American inventor George Devol was the first to design a robot that could be programmed to do different tasks. About 20 years later, Wabot-1 was created in Tokyo, Japan. Wabot-1 could see, grasp, walk, and speak a few words.

▼ *George Devol worked on the programmable robot, Unimate, shown here filling bottles of lotion; one of the many tasks it could perform.*

sensors: devices that recognize something by one of the five senses

Robots at Work

First Robots on the Job

Some jobs are extremely dangerous and even impossible for humans to do. Others are too disgustingly dirty, or too boring for humans. Twentieth-century robots became the answer to the problem: who will do the work that nobody wants to do?

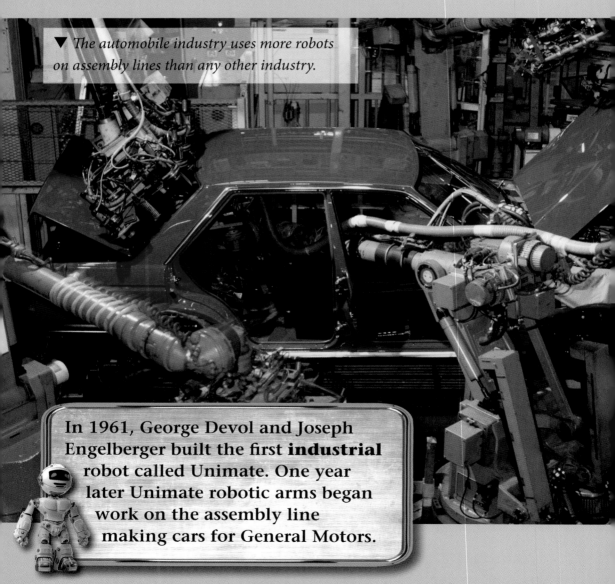

▼ *The automobile industry uses more robots on assembly lines than any other industry.*

In 1961, George Devol and Joseph Engelberger built the first **industrial** robot called Unimate. One year later Unimate robotic arms began work on the assembly line making cars for General Motors.

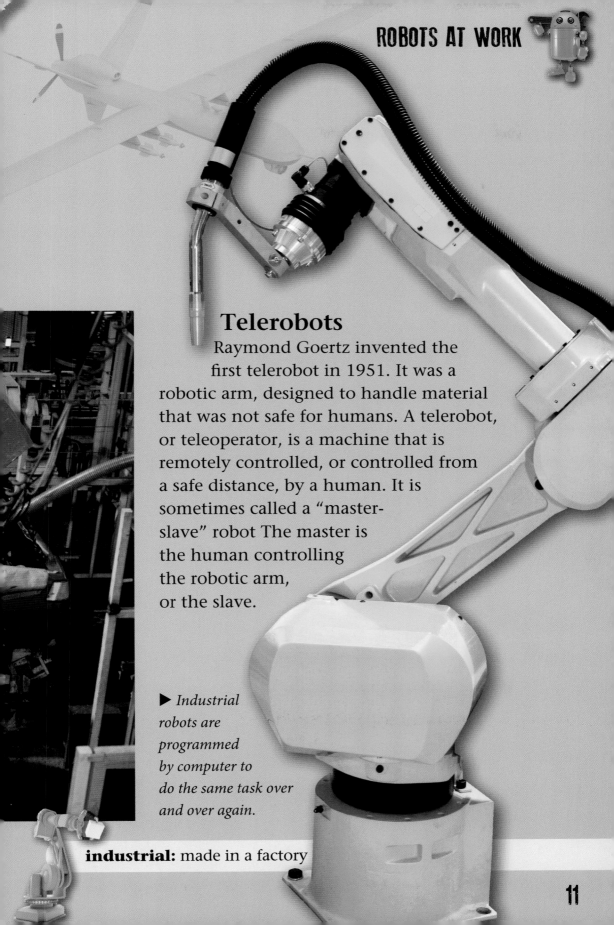

Telerobots

Raymond Goertz invented the first telerobot in 1951. It was a robotic arm, designed to handle material that was not safe for humans. A telerobot, or teleoperator, is a machine that is remotely controlled, or controlled from a safe distance, by a human. It is sometimes called a "master-slave" robot The master is the human controlling the robotic arm, or the slave.

▶ *Industrial robots are programmed by computer to do the same task over and over again.*

industrial: made in a factory

11

On the Assembly Line

Industrial robots repeat the same job over and over again, and never get tired or bored. They can work 24 hours a day and never need breaks, take vacations, or get sick. They work faster and have greater strength than people—and they almost never make mistakes.

▼ *Robots can do precise tasks endlessly, and can be designed to fit in spaces that human hands never could.*

A Million Robots

But everything wears out in time, and robots do need to be checked to see that they are working properly, or fixed if they break down. Most industrial robots that work on assembly lines are **stationary** and have one or more working arms. In 2014, there were over 1 million working industrial robots on Earth!

A robot's ability to move is called its degree of freedom (DOF). It is a measurement of the number of twists, turns, or rolls it can do.

▼ *Although robots do not get sick days off from work; there is the rare time that they may need a few repairs and maintenance.*

stationary: staying in one place

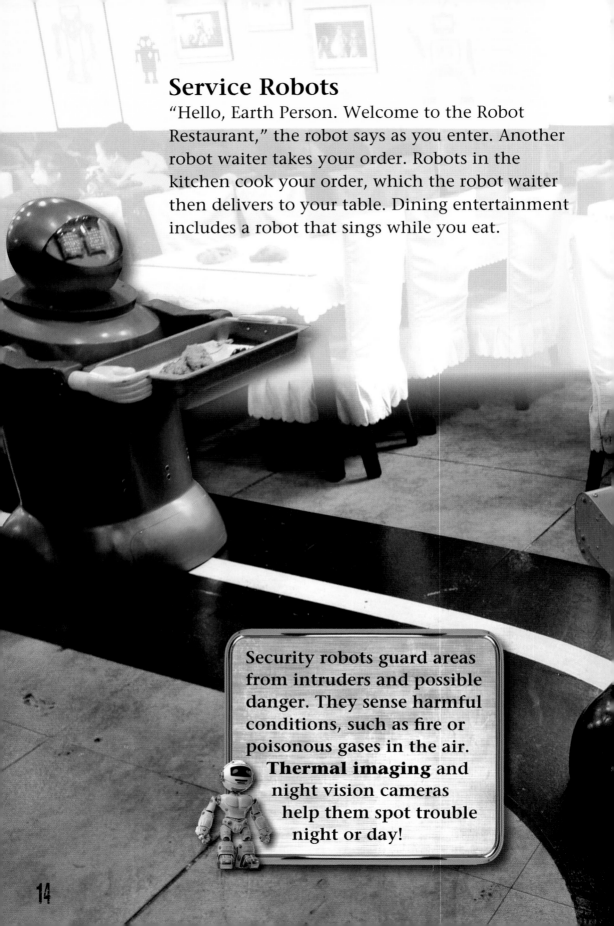

Service Robots

"Hello, Earth Person. Welcome to the Robot Restaurant," the robot says as you enter. Another robot waiter takes your order. Robots in the kitchen cook your order, which the robot waiter then delivers to your table. Dining entertainment includes a robot that sings while you eat.

Security robots guard areas from intruders and possible danger. They sense harmful conditions, such as fire or poisonous gases in the air. **Thermal imaging** and night vision cameras help them spot trouble night or day!

Robot Restaurant

Although it might sound like something from the distant future, restaurants staffed with robot workers first opened in China in 2009. Service robots can work for five hours before needing to recharge. Each service robot costs over $40,000. Other restaurants around the world are looking to employ robots in the near future for cooking and serving.

◄ *Robots today greet and serve customers in restaurants, and can even cook the meal!*

thermal imaging: using an object's heat to make a picture of it

Taking Over the Tough Jobs

KUKA Titan is a heavyweight champion of industrial robots. The robotic stationary arm lifts objects that weigh over 2,200 pounds (998 kilograms) effortlessly. Objects such as cars or cement staircases that are usually handled by cranes are no problem for this much smaller, but mightier, industrial arm.

▲ *Farm robots lighten farmers' loads by doing tasks such as harvesting, caring for crops, and milking cows. This automatic milker uses a laser to find the cow's teats and can milk a herd without human help.*

Mechanical Milking

In the past, a dairy cow had to wait for the farmer to milk her. But today, she decides when she will be milked. She walks right into the Lely Astronaut A4 milking robot. While the robot milks her, she eats a treat of some grains. Life is good—even for a cow— with robot helpers.

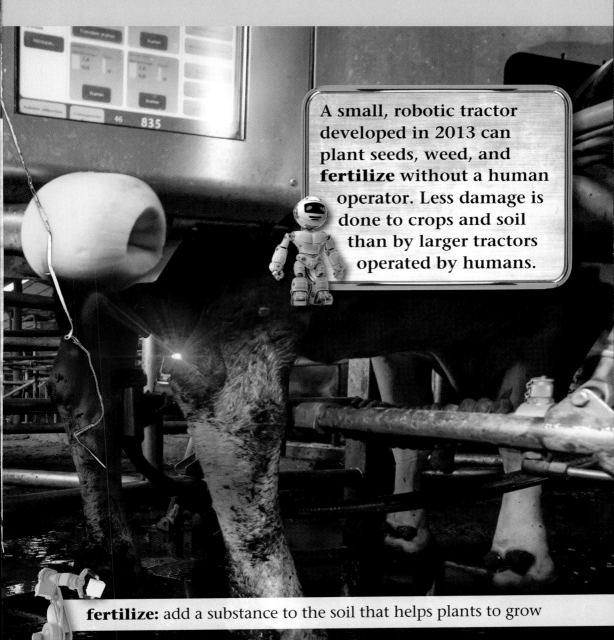

A small, robotic tractor developed in 2013 can plant seeds, weed, and **fertilize** without a human operator. Less damage is done to crops and soil than by larger tractors operated by humans.

fertilize: add a substance to the soil that helps plants to grow

Robots in Space

Robots Are Out of This World!

During the 1950s, robots were a popular theme in books and movies. American author Isaac Asimov published a book of **sci-fi** short stories called *I, Robot* in 1950. Asimov's Three Laws of Robotics, found in *I, Robot*, are still referred to today in television shows such as *The Simpsons* and movies such as *I, Robot* (2004).

► *Asimov was inspired by this 1938 story. Unusually, the robot was the story's hero, not its villain.*

Asimov's Three Laws of Robotics are:
1. Robots cannot harm humans or allow a human to be harmed.
2. Robots must obey orders given by humans, unless it involves harming other humans.
3. Robots must protect themselves from harm unless it conflicts with Laws 1 and 2.

18

Science Fiction or Science Fact?

The Day the Earth Stood Still was a popular movie in 1951. It was about an alien named Klaatu and his robot Gort, who travel to Earth in a spaceship. Over 60 years later, human-designed robots are traveling through space to visit other planets. But, this time, it's for real!

▶ *Robby the Robot was a character in the 1956 movie* Forbidden Planet. *Movie robots in the 1950s weren't real; they were actors in robot costumes.*

sci-fi: science fiction, made-up stories about the future

Robots Working in Space

Lunokhod was the first robot in space. The eight-wheeled, robotic rover landed on the moon on November 17, 1970. This hard-working robot traveled more than 6 miles (9 kilometers), took more than 20,000 images, and tested the moon's soil for 11 months.

▼ *These stamps show Lunokhod on the moon. The word* Lunokhod *means "moon walker" in Russian.*

Canadarm

The Canadarm is another first for robotics in space. This Canadian-designed robotic arm was first put to work aboard the *Columbia* STS-2 space shuttle on November 13, 1981. Since then, the six-jointed arm has solved a number of problems in space such as breaking dangerous ice off shuttles and repairing the Hubble Space Telescope.

▲ *The Canadarm2 grabs and moves heavy objects in space. It has 7 DOF (see page 13) and is over 55 feet (17 meters) long.*

"[The Canadarm] was like an **extension** of your own arm. I [loved] how neat it was, how much like the human arm it was … It was my first exposure to real robotics."

Space Shuttle STS-2 Mission commander, Joe Engle

extension: a part that is added to something to make it longer

21

Missions to Mars

Scientists have long wondered if people could live on Mars. But it is too dangerous and expensive to send astronauts. NASA decided to send the next best thing— robots! Sojourner rover was the first to explore Mars in 1997. Spirit and Opportunity followed in 2003. Curiosity landed in 2012.

The latest Mars rover, Curiosity, landed on Mars in August 2012. Curiosity is equipped with sensors that read weather conditions and **radiation** levels present on Mars.

Roving Robots

Mars Exploration rovers have special tools that help investigate the surface of Mars. The rock abrasion tool (RAT) can dig into hard rock. A robotic arm and magnets help collect soil samples. The magnets attract and collect magnetic dust found in the air on Mars. Cameras take close-up images of samples. Scientific tools called spectrometers analyze samples to see what they are made of.

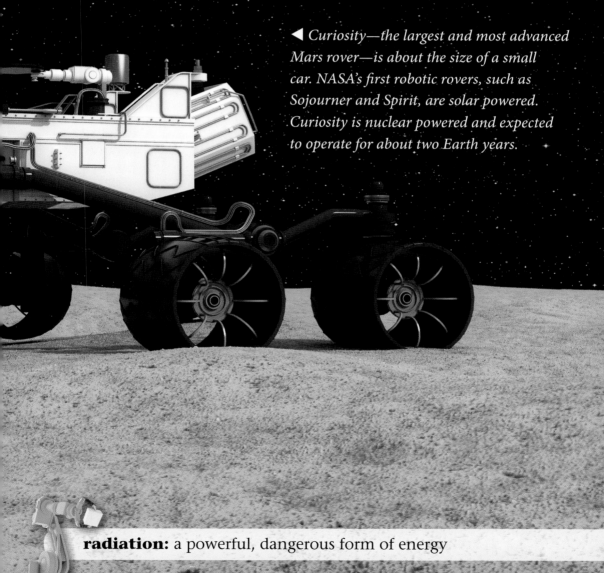

◀ Curiosity—the largest and most advanced Mars rover—is about the size of a small car. NASA's first robotic rovers, such as Sojourner and Spirit, are solar powered. Curiosity is nuclear powered and expected to operate for about two Earth years.

radiation: a powerful, dangerous form of energy

Future Robots in Space

An insect-like robot flies from the back of a Mars rover. It has twin wings, one fluttering on the front and another on the back. It quickly flies close to the planet's surface. It slows down and hovers over an interesting rock. A small arm extends to take a sample. Drawing the arm back inside its body, it quickly flies back to the rover to bring the rock sample for study and to refuel.

NASA is designing robotic flight landers or spacecraft that will help explore other planets and moons. The Mighty Eagle— named after an Angry Birds game character!—is small, smart, and will quickly gather images and samples from outer space in the near future.

▲ *Sometimes the best ideas can be found in nature. Some robots, such as the entomopter, are designed to move and fly as insects do.*

Entomopters on Mars?

This insect-like robot is called an entomopter. "Entomo" means insect. NASA is working toward designing a more advanced entomopter robot that could fly over difficult areas and through the thin air of the Martian **atmosphere**.

▼ *The rocky surface of Mars can make problems for land rovers. A flying entomopter could cover Mars's surface more quickly and easily than a land vehicle.*

atmosphere: the gases that surround a planet

A Soldier's Best Friend

American soldiers wait outside a building where they believe enemy soldiers are inside. If they entered, they could be shot, or it could be **booby-trapped** with a bomb. One soldier takes a Packbot 510 from his backpack. He sets up a laptop computer and operates the robot with a videogame controller. Packbot 510 searches the building on tracks attached to a belt that rotates around wheels. The Packbot 510 can search for enemy soldiers and explosives.

◀ *These paratroopers are being trained to use the Packbot.*

Helping to Save Lives

Packbot 510 is only one of a number of robots that help save lives in the military. Cameras send images back to a soldier's laptop. It is equipped with thermal imaging. Thermal imaging uses the heat that an object or living thing gives off to help them see in the dark. Sensors sniff out bombs, chemical poisons, or radiation.

▼ *After Japan's earthquake in 2011, Packbot 510 worked inside the damaged nuclear power plant because the leaking radiation was too dangerous for people.*

"**Packbot fulfilled a mission that flesh-and-bones soldiers, risking life and limb, used to do... More than 750 such robots have been lost in combat in Iraq and Afghanistan—a number that translates into many saved lives.**"

The Wall Street Journal, 2012

booby-trapped: set with a trap, such as a bomb or explosive device

Emergency!

Battlefields are one of the most dangerous places to be. Soldiers in combat are fighting for their lives. But what happens if a soldier is shot, injured, and cannot move to safety or get medical attention? Another person coming in to save the injured soldier would also risk getting shot.

Bear to the Rescue

The Bear, created by Vecna, is a new disaster recovery robot that could help in this situation. "Bear" stands for Battlefield **Extraction**-Assist Robot. The Bear is designed to locate, lift, and carry a person or other heavy item, without risking other people's lives to do so.

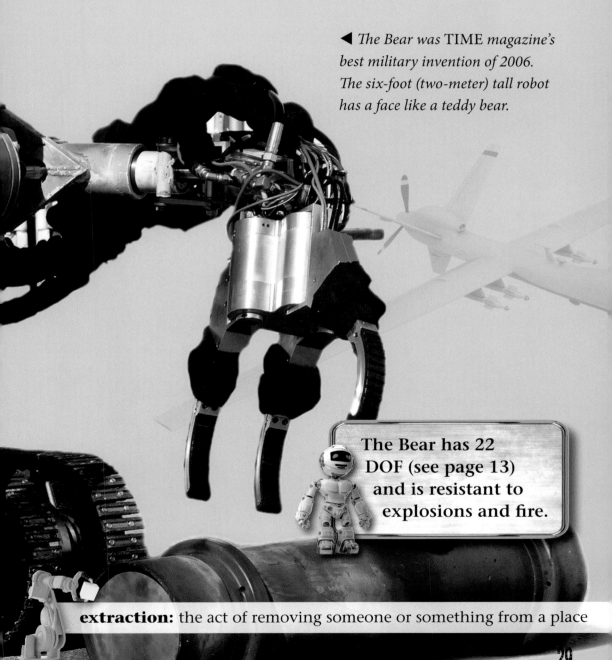

◄ *The Bear was* TIME *magazine's best military invention of 2006. The six-foot (two-meter) tall robot has a face like a teddy bear.*

The Bear has 22 DOF (see page 13) and is resistant to explosions and fire.

extraction: the act of removing someone or something from a place

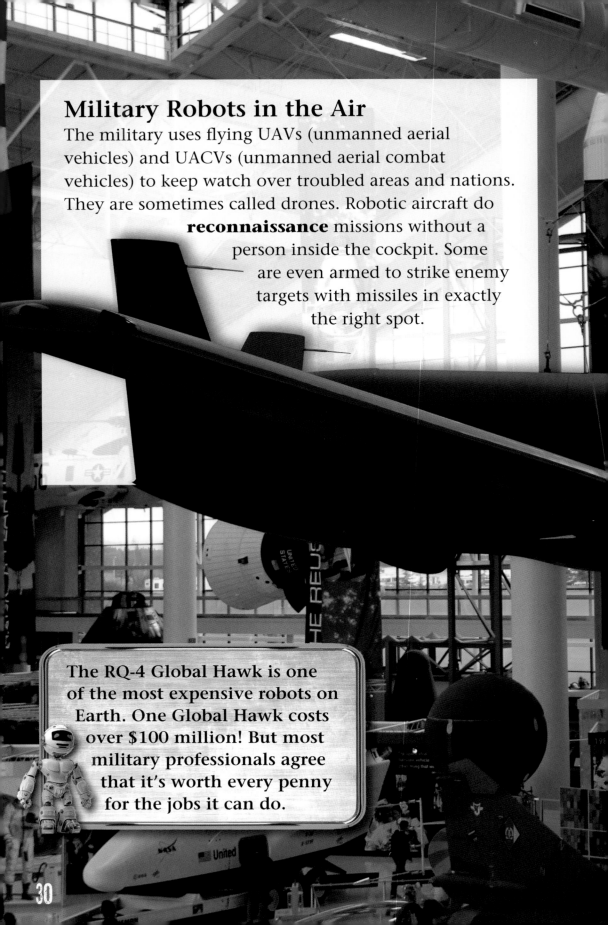

Military Robots in the Air

The military uses flying UAVs (unmanned aerial vehicles) and UACVs (unmanned aerial combat vehicles) to keep watch over troubled areas and nations. They are sometimes called drones. Robotic aircraft do **reconnaissance** missions without a person inside the cockpit. Some are even armed to strike enemy targets with missiles in exactly the right spot.

The RQ-4 Global Hawk is one of the most expensive robots on Earth. One Global Hawk costs over $100 million! But most military professionals agree that it's worth every penny for the jobs it can do.

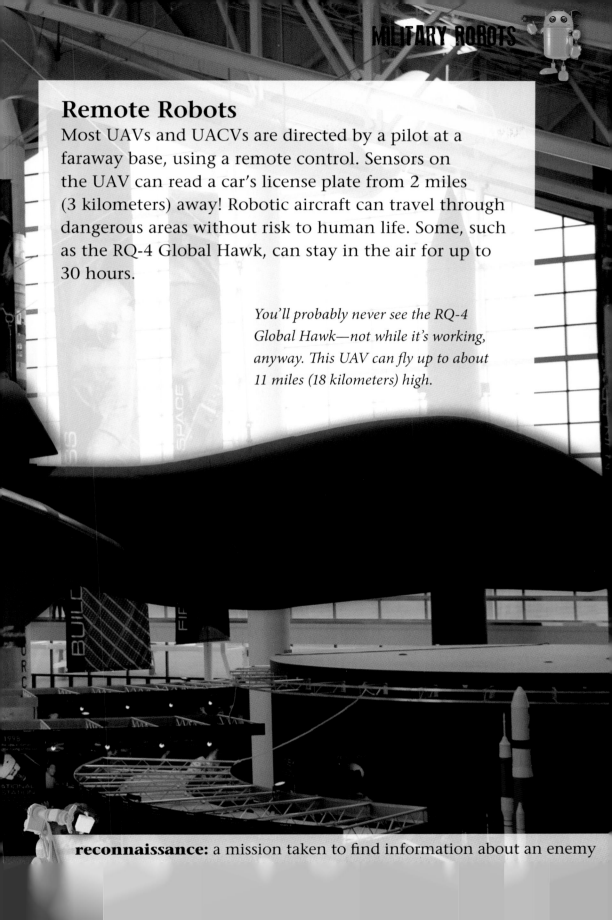

Remote Robots

Most UAVs and UACVs are directed by a pilot at a faraway base, using a remote control. Sensors on the UAV can read a car's license plate from 2 miles (3 kilometers) away! Robotic aircraft can travel through dangerous areas without risk to human life. Some, such as the RQ-4 Global Hawk, can stay in the air for up to 30 hours.

You'll probably never see the RQ-4 Global Hawk—not while it's working, anyway. This UAV can fly up to about 11 miles (18 kilometers) high.

reconnaissance: a mission taken to find information about an enemy

Difficult Operation

Pat had cancer. A tumor, or growth, at the base of his tongue had to be removed. It was a risky operation—a human surgeon would have to saw Pat's lower jaw in half to get at the tumor to remove it. Even if the operation went well, Pat would be left with a large scar on his throat and many weeks of painful recovery.

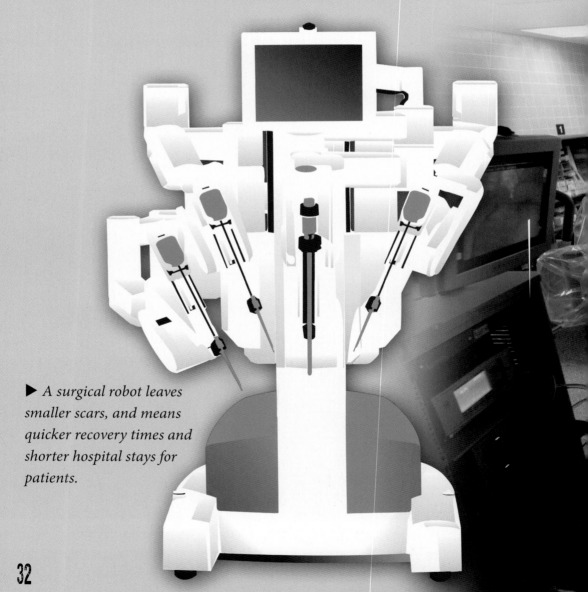

▶ A surgical robot leaves smaller scars, and means quicker recovery times and shorter hospital stays for patients.

Robot Surgeon

Pat and his doctor decided to use a groundbreaking new surgical robot called da Vinci instead. The da Vinci robot's smaller surgical instruments would be able to reach the tumor by going in through Pat's mouth. The instruments would be guided by the human surgeon's hand movements on a controller. The surgery was over in less than half an hour without having to cut through Pat's jawbone.

Microbots and nanobots are tiny robots that do medical tasks that humans cannot do. The Norika3 is a robot that a patient swallows. The capsule releases a camera that moves through a person's **digestive system** and takes images.

◄ *This surgeon is using the da Vinci robot to assist with heart surgery.*

digestive system: the part of the body that breaks down food

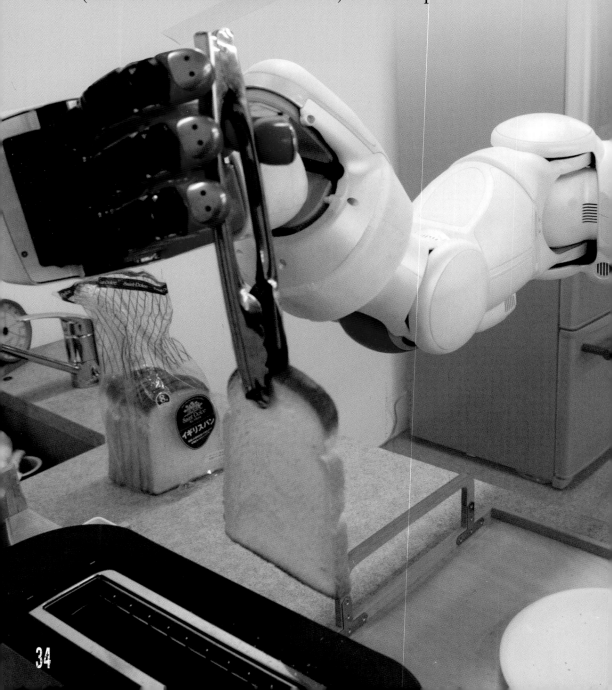

Nurse-bots

Natalie is an elderly person with a **disability**. Natalie's relatives worry that something might happen to her while she's home alone, and she won't be able to call for help. They want her to move into a nursing home, but Natalie does not want to go there. Nurse-bots (the short form for nurse-robots) could help.

Robotic Bedside Manners

Nurse-bots are robots that help care for older or disabled people. A nurse-bot can lift a person from their bed into a wheelchair. Nurse-bots can also do tasks such as make meals, or carry household items. They can remind people when to take their medicine or when to eat or drink.

◄ *This nurse-bot is called Twendy-One. Researchers feel that making nurse-bots look more human will make patients like them better.*

Nurse-bots provide their patients with telepresence. Telepresence allows people who are not together to see and communicate with each other by computer screens. Patients could visit with healthcare givers, relatives, or others through this technology.

disability: a condition that limits what a person can do

Human-like Robots

"You're adorable," says Cynthia to a robotic head named Kismet. Kismet responds by making a facial expression of happiness like a child. Kismet's facial features (eyes, eyebrows, neck, lips, and ears) each have two or more DOF (see page 13). These allow Kismet to show emotions such as happiness, sadness, disgust, excitement, anger, surprise—just about any emotion a human face can show.

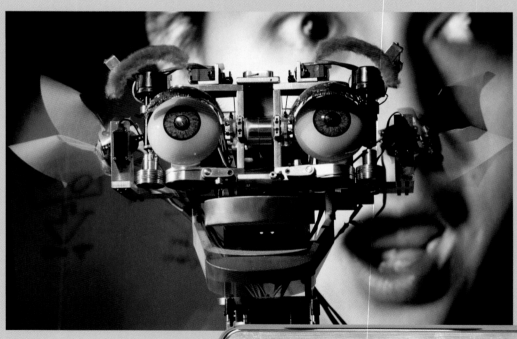

▲ *Kismet (shown here) was designed by roboticist professor Cynthia Breazeal (image shown behind Kismet) in the late 1990s. Cynthia created Kismet to further investigate how humans interact with robots.*

Kismet is a robot with artificial intelligence. Artificial intelligence is the ability of something made by humans, such as a robot, to interact with people in an intelligent and "human" manner.

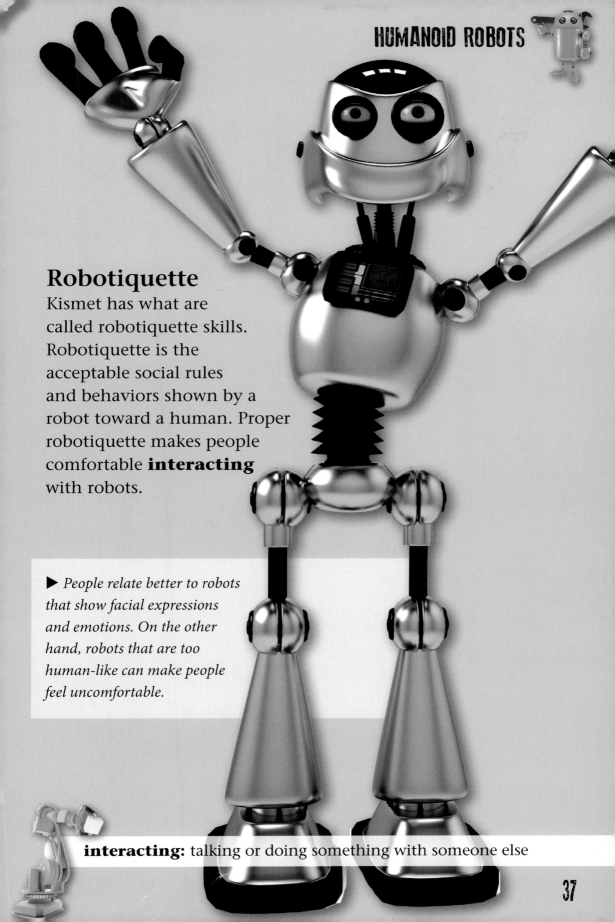

Robotiquette

Kismet has what are called robotiquette skills. Robotiquette is the acceptable social rules and behaviors shown by a robot toward a human. Proper robotiquette makes people comfortable **interacting** with robots.

▶ *People relate better to robots that show facial expressions and emotions. On the other hand, robots that are too human-like can make people feel uncomfortable.*

interacting: talking or doing something with someone else

Humans vs. Humanoids?

It is the year 2050. Two soccer teams
face each other on the field: the
World Cup soccer champions vs. the
RoboCup soccer champions. One is a
team of athletic young men. The other
is a team of **humanoid**
robots. Who will win?
Only time will tell.

"Robots are made to do special jobs. And
what they must be able to do is perform
those special tasks a thousand times
better than a human so that we benefit."

Hiroaki Kitano, artificial intelligence specialist
and founder of RoboCup

◄ *The official goal of RoboCup is to design a team of humanoid robot soccer players that will defeat the human World Cup soccer champions by 2050!*

Sporty Robots

The RoboCup is the most famous competition between robots in the world. This robot soccer game is a lot slower-paced than a human soccer game. The robot players on each team are not able to run. They can only walk forward, sideways, and kick the ball. Sometimes they fall over, but they can get up by themselves. But, even in soccer, robotics is quickly improving!

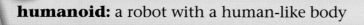

humanoid: a robot with a human-like body

Extreme Robots

Hot Spot

In 1992, a volcano erupted at Mount Spurr, Alaska. Volcanic craters are one of Earth's most dangerous environments. In the past, scientists collected high-temperature gas samples from volcanoes to study them further. But it is a dangerous job. Eight scientists died in 1993 during two separate events while sampling volcanoes. A team from NASA designed a robot called Dante II that would measure dangerous volcanic activity instead of sending a human to do the job.

▲ Dante II's exploration of a volcano crater included traveling along steep walls to the volcano floor. Scientists used Dante II's journey to research how to build other robots to explore other planets in the future.

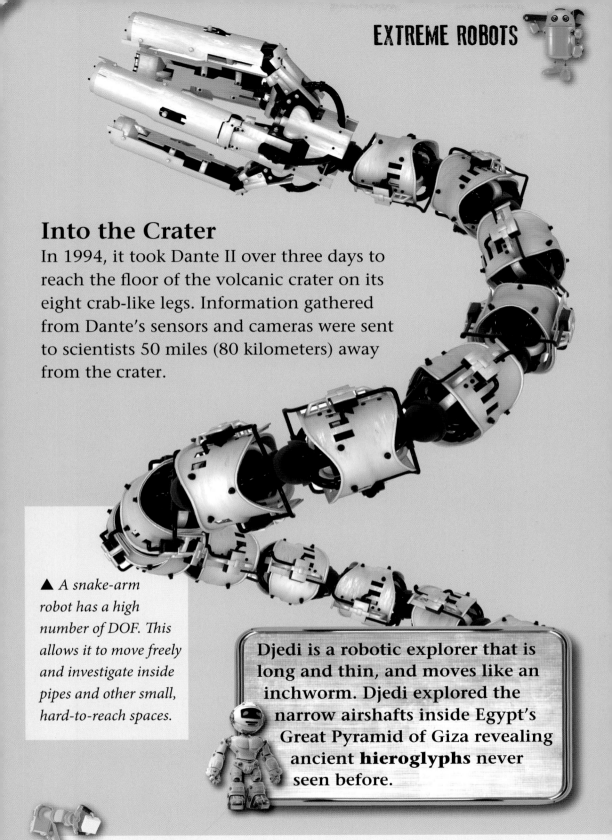

Into the Crater

In 1994, it took Dante II over three days to reach the floor of the volcanic crater on its eight crab-like legs. Information gathered from Dante's sensors and cameras were sent to scientists 50 miles (80 kilometers) away from the crater.

▲ *A snake-arm robot has a high number of DOF. This allows it to move freely and investigate inside pipes and other small, hard-to-reach spaces.*

Djedi is a robotic explorer that is long and thin, and moves like an inchworm. Djedi explored the narrow airshafts inside Egypt's Great Pyramid of Giza revealing ancient **hieroglyphs** never seen before.

hieroglyphs: pictures or symbols used to represent words or sounds

41

Underwater Robots

Air France Flight 447 tragically crashed into the Atlantic Ocean off South America in 2009. Its whereabouts remained a mystery for about two years. In 2011, an AUV (**autonomous** underwater vehicle) spotted and photographed AF Flight 447's wreckage located more than 2 miles (3 kilometers) underwater. Humans cannot withstand the pressure underwater at the depths that robots can.

◄ *Underwater robotic submarines can explore deep-sea areas that humans cannot safely reach. Some ROVs (remotely operated vehicles) dive more than 6 miles (9 kilometers) underwater.*

"... this new technology of submersibles and robots can now cover ninety-seven percent of the world's oceans ... There's probably more history now preserved underwater than in all the museums of the world combined."

Robert Ballard, who discovered the shipwreck of *Titanic* in 1985

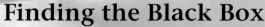

Finding the Black Box

Another robotic submarine called the Remora 6000 was sent down to find the plane's flight data recorder, called the black box. Using its two arms and color cameras, the Remora 6000 was able to recover the black box and help solve the mystery of why the plane went down. The plane was going too slowly, stalled in the air, and fell into the ocean.

▲ *AUVs—such as the Seahorse shown here—are used by the U.S. Navy to see and explore underwater areas that cannot be reached by humans.*

autonomous: able to act independently

Robots Today

In 2004, a World Robot Declaration statement was released. It stated that: "Next-generation robots will be partners that **coexist** with human beings ... Next-generation robots will contribute to the realization of a safe and peaceful society."

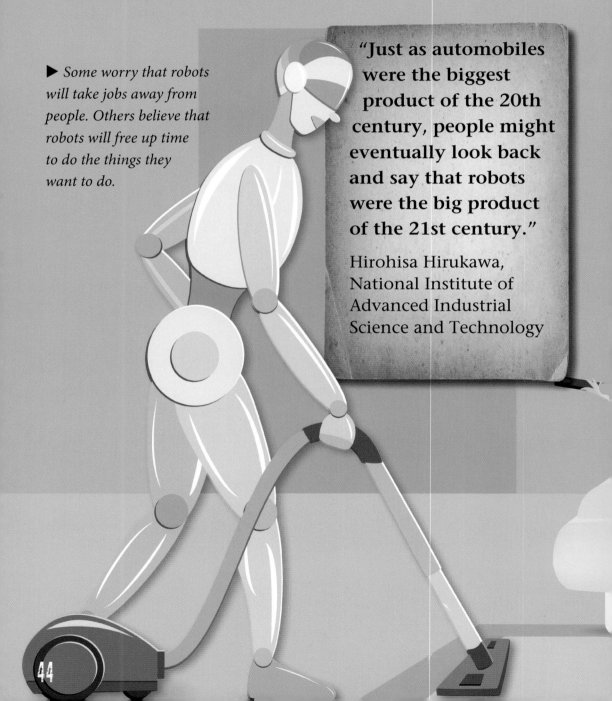

▶ *Some worry that robots will take jobs away from people. Others believe that robots will free up time to do the things they want to do.*

"Just as automobiles were the biggest product of the 20th century, people might eventually look back and say that robots were the big product of the 21st century."

Hirohisa Hirukawa, National Institute of Advanced Industrial Science and Technology

Robots in the Future

Scientists are already working on nanobots that are even more advanced. Others are working on robotic parts that can replace human limbs and other body parts. Robotic technology is always advancing. Who knows what robots will be capable of doing for humans in the future?

Timeline

1948 William Grey Walter invents a robotic tortoise with sensors.

1961 George Devol and Joseph Engelberger create the first industrial robot, Unimate.

November 17, 1970 The first robotic rover, Lunokhod, lands on the Moon.

November 13, 1981 The robotic arm, Canadarm, is used on the first space flight.

1997 The robotic rover Sojourner explores Mars.

2003 The robotic rovers Spirit and Opportunity explore Mars.

2011 An AUV discovers Air France Flight 447 at the bottom of the Atlantic Ocean.

2012 The robotic rover Curiosity explores Mars.

2034 The estimated date when most households will be cleaned, managed, and cared for by robots.

coexist: live alongside each other

Learning More

Books

Robot
by Roger Bridgman
(DK Children, 2004)

Robots
by Clive Gifford
(Atheneum Books for Young Readers, 2008)

Robots
by Melissa Stewart
(National Geographic Readers, 2014)

Websites

http://mars.jpl.nasa.gov/msl/mission/instruments/environsensors/rems/Check out the weather on Mars through the robotic rover, Curiosity

www.sciencekids.co.nz/robots.html
Robots for kids website includes games, facts, projects, quizzes, videos and more

www.thetech.org/exhibits/online/robotics/index.html
A great learning resource for students with history, art, and more

www.pbs.org/wgbh/nova/robots/
A PBS site that explores future robots, dangerous duty robots, and videos of robots in action

Glossary

atmosphere The gases that surround a planet

automaton (plural: automata) A moving machine, often in the shape of a human

autonomous Able to act independently

booby-trapped Set with a trap, such as a bomb or explosive device

coexist Live alongside each other

diagnosed Found out what was wrong with someone

digestive system The part of the body that breaks down food

disability A condition that limits what a person can do

extension A part that is added to something to make it longer

extraction The act of removing someone or something from a place

fertilize Add a substance to the soil that helps plants to grow

hieroglyphs Pictures or symbols used to represent words or sounds

humanoid A robot with a human-like body

industrial Made in a factory

interacting Talking or doing something with someone else

radiation A powerful, dangerous form of energy

reconnaissance A mission taken to find information about an enemy

sci-fi Science fiction, made-up stories about the future

sensors Devices that recognize something by one of the five senses

stationary Staying in one place

thermal imaging Using an object's heat to make a picture of it

Index

Entries in **bold** refer to pictures